~~THOMPS...~~
# RACING
# CARS

This book is officially licensed by Winning Moves UK Ltd,
owners of the Top Trumps registered trademark.

Andrew Van de Burgt has asserted his right to be identified as the
author of this book.

British Library Cataloguing-in-Publication Data:
A catalogue record for this book is available from the British Library

ISBN 1 84425 397 X

Library of Congress catalog card no. 2006928056

Published by Haynes Publishing,
Sparkford, Yeovil, Somerset BA22 7JJ, UK
Tel: 01963 442030 Fax: 01963 440001
Int. tel: +44 1963 442030 Int. fax: +44 1963 440001
Email: sales@haynes.co.uk
Website: www.haynes.co.uk

Haynes North America, Inc.,
861 Lawrence Drive, Newbury Park
California 91320, USA

Printed and bound in Great Britain by
J. H. Haynes & Co. Ltd, Sparkford

**Photographic credits**: algp.com; BMW Sauber; BTCC.com; Ebrey/
Lola; F3euroseries; GP2series.com; GPM/Gettyimages; Honda Racing;
IRL IndyCar; Ishihara; LAT Photographic; Red Bull Racing; Renault;
Renault F1; rprincephoto.com; SLC; Spyker; Williams F1.

## The Author

Andrew Van de Burgt is editor of *Autosport*, travelling to most of the
Grands Prix, and is a lifelong motor racing enthusiast.

# TOP TRUMPS®
## RACING CARS

# Contents

# About
# Top Trumps

It's now more than 30 years since Britain's kids first caught the Top Trumps craze. The game remained hugely popular until the 1990s, when it slowly drifted into obscurity. Then, in 1999, UK games company Winning Moves discovered it, bought it, dusted it down, gave it a thorough makeover and introduced it to a whole new generation. And so the Top Trumps legend continues.

Nowadays, there are Top Trumps titles for just about everyone, with subjects about animals, cars, ships, aircraft and all the great films and TV shows. Top Trumps is now even more popular than before. In Britain, a pack of Top Trumps is bought every six seconds! And it's not just British children who love the game. Children in Australasia, the Far East, the Middle East, all over Europe and in North America can buy Top Trumps at their local shops.

Today you can even play the game on the internet, interactive DVD, your games console and even your mobile phone.

## You've played the game...

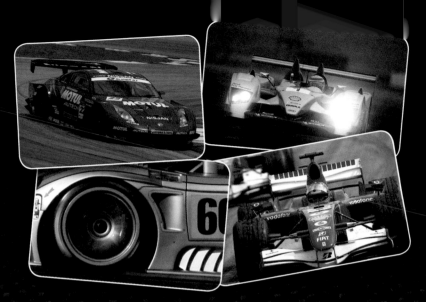

# Now read the book!

Haynes Publishing and Top Trumps have teamed up to bring you this exciting new Top Trumps book, in which you will find even more pictures, details and statistics.

**Top Trumps: Racing Cars** features 45 of the world's most exciting modern racing cars, from the current Formula 1 top-rankers to stateside NASCAR muscle and the endurance stars of Le Mans. Packed with fascinating facts, stunning photographs and all the vital statistics, this is the essential pocket guide. And if you're lucky enough to spot any of these racing cars, then at the back of the book we've provided space for you to record when and where you saw them.

Look out for other Top Trumps books from Haynes Publishing – even more facts, even more fun!

# WTCC
# Alfa Romeo 156

**Privateers keep historic name alive**

betandwin
G.Morbidelli
ADVAN
16
KW suspension.de
MAHLE
BOSCH
TRW
ADVAN

# WTCC

# AlFa Romeo 156

**Privateers keep historic name alive**

Alfa Romeo is one of the world's most evocative car manufacturers, with a long and illustrious history of success across many branches of motor racing. The works Alfas, built by Italian engineers N-Technology, were BMW's fiercest rivals in the European Touring Car Championship, the forerunner to the World Championship. Despite coming close to the 2005 title, the Alfa 156 was getting long in the tooth and at board level Alfa dithered over the decision to turn its replacement, the 159, into a Super 2000 racer for the WTCC. Time finally ran out and Alfa withdrew from the series. However, N-Technology felt the 156 still had something to offer and opted to run the cars as an independent. With talented young Brazilian Augusto Farfus Jr, joined in the team by veteran ex-Ferrari Formula 1 racer Gianni Morbidelli, the 156 was still a force to be reckoned with, but without works support it failed to challenge consistently.

## Statistics

| | |
|---|---|
| **Chassis:** | Tubular steel frame |
| **Engine size:** | 1998cc |
| **Configuration:** | In-line four |
| **Bhp:** | 274bhp |
| **Max rpm:** | 7000rpm |
| **Top speed:** | 160mph |
| **0-60mph:** | 4.2sec |
| **Weight:** | 1140kg (inc driver) |
| **Gearbox:** | Six-speed sequential |
| **Fuel:** | Unleaded |
| **Tyres:** | Yokohama |
| **Wheels:** | 17in rims |
| **Front suspension:** | Double wishbone with gas-filled dampers |
| **Rear suspension:** | McPherson strut with gas-filled dampers |
| **Brakes:** | Steel discs with carbon pads |

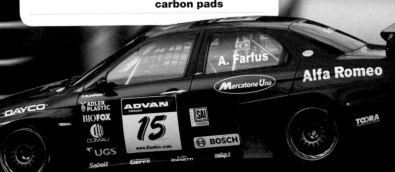

## FIA GT
# Aston Martin DBR9
**Taking British Racing Green back to the front**

# FIA GT

# Aston Martin DBR9

**Taking British Racing Green back to the front**

The DBR9 is Aston Martin's fabulous-looking re-entry into GT racing. Developed by British aces Prodrive, the car made an instant impact after its 2005 launch by winning its class first time out in the classic Sebring 12 hours endurance race. Not only is the DBR9 a potent racer, it is also highly exclusive, with only 12 of the works-supported cars built, although in total around 30 are in existence. The DBR name pays homage to Aston Martin's 1959 Le Mans winner, the DBR1, and success in the historic 24-hour race is one of the company's main aims. Although the car is visually similar to the road-going version – and follows the same dimensions – it has been re-engineered for racing, with lightweight materials used wherever possible. Power is provided by an all-aluminium V12 engine derived from the road car version, producing a whopping 600-plus horsepower.

# Statistics

| | |
|---|---|
| Chassis: | Aluminium chassis with carbon-fibre bodywork |
| Engine size: | 6000cc |
| Configuration: | V12 |
| Bhp: | 600bhp |
| Max rpm: | n/a |
| Top speed: | 202mph |
| 0-60mph: | 3.8sec |
| Weight: | 1100kg (FIA GT) |
| Gearbox: | Six-speed sequential |
| Fuel: | Unleaded |
| Tyres: | Michelin |
| Wheels: | OZ 19in rims |
| Front suspension: | Double wishbone with adjustable dampers |
| Rear suspension: | Double wishbone with adjustable dampers |
| Brakes: | Carbon-fibre discs and pads front and rear |

# DTM
# Audi A4

**Audi's ultimate V8 touring car**

# DTM
# Audi A4

**Audi's ultimate V8 touring car**

Audi entered the DTM as a works force in 2004 and instantly won the title. For the previous three seasons, the privateer ABT outfit had run elongated TTs in the pan-European series, winning the 2002 title, but the arrival of the official works teams heralded a switch to the four-door A4. ABT was kept on as one of the supported teams, while crack sportscar outfit Joest also ran the V8-powered cars. ABT was the more successful of the two and was entrusted with running the new 2005-spec cars, while Joest campaigned the year-old models. Mattias Ekstrom came close to claiming back-to-back titles, but was pipped at the final round. Following the specification freeze for 2006, the latest A4 is a subtle improvement on the 2005 car and, like Mercedes, Audi has expanded to a 10-car team, with a plethora of 2005 and 2004 cars making up the numbers following the withdrawal of the works Opel team.

| | |
|---|---|
| **Chassis:** | **Tubular spaceframe** |
| **Engine size:** | **4000cc** |
| **Configuration:** | **90-degree V8** |
| **Bhp:** | **460bhp** |
| **Max rpm:** | **7000rpm** |
| **Top speed:** | **170mph** |
| **0-60mph:** | **3.6sec** |
| **Weight:** | **1070kg** |
| **Gearbox:** | **Six-speed sequential** |
| **Fuel:** | **Unleaded** |
| **Tyres:** | **Dunlop** |
| **Wheels:** | **OZ** |
| **Front suspension:** | **Double wishbone with adjustable dampers** |
| **Rear suspension:** | **Double wishbone with adjustable dampers** |
| **Brakes:** | **Carbon-fibre discs front and rear** |

# Le Mans
# Audi R10

**Diesel power for sportscar greats**

# Le Mans
# Audi R10

**Diesel power for sportscar greats**

In recent years, Audi has ruled sportscar racing, with its magnificent R8 taking countless titles in Europe and America, as well as an amazing five victories in the world-famous Le Mans 24 Hours. Yet despite the R8 still being a front-running package, Audi introduced the stunning R10 for 2006. With its silver and red corporate livery, the car takes its styling cues from the R8, but under closer inspection it's clear this is indeed a sophisticated and thoroughly modern racer, built in conjunction with Italian chassis aces Dallara. But it's not the high-tech chassis that sets this car apart, but its unique diesel engine. With diesels now making up almost half of Europe's road car sales, Audi saw the R10 as a perfect proving ground for its diesel engine technology. And with the 5.5-litre V12 pumping out over 650bhp, there's no chance of unfavourably comparing this racer to a tractor, as used to be the case with old-fashioned diesels!

# Statistics

| | |
|---|---|
| **Chassis:** | **Carbon-fibre monocoque** |
| **Engine size:** | **5500cc** |
| **Configuration:** | **90-degree V12 twin turbo** |
| **Bhp:** | **700bhp** |
| **Max rpm:** | **7500rpm** |
| **Top speed:** | **220mph** |
| **0-60mph:** | **2.8sec** |
| **Weight:** | **925kg** |
| **Gearbox:** | **Five-speed sequential** |
| **Fuel:** | **Shell diesel** |
| **Tyres:** | **Michelin** |
| **Wheels:** | **18in rims** |
| **Front suspension:** | **Double wishbone with adjustable dampers** |
| **Rear suspension:** | **Double wishbone with adjustable dampers** |
| **Brakes:** | **Carbon-fibre discs front and rear** |

# WTCC
# BMW 320si

**Four-door world beater**

# BMW 320si

**Four-door world beater**

BMW is the king of world touring cars. The German manufacturer won the one-off world title in 1987 and when the championship was reborn in 2005 it won again. Not content to rest of its laurels, a new model has been introduced this year in the shape of the 320si, which takes the body shape of the latest 3-series road car range, but breaks from BMW's recent touring car heritage by using a four-cylinder engine rather than the traditional straight six. The World Touring Car Championship runs to Super 2000 touring car regulations. This means the cars retain the outward appearance of their road car cousins and also employ the same suspension layout and engine position. BMW's unique rear-wheel-drive philosophy gives the 320si a natural rear weight bias, which makes the cars almost unbeatable off the line. This has helped 2005 world champ Andy Priaulx and fellow works BMW stars Jorg Muller, Dirk Muller, Alex Zanardi and Marcel Costa to keep up the marque's superb record.

# Statistics

| | |
|---|---|
| **Chassis:** | **Tubular steel frame** |
| **Engine size:** | **1998cc** |
| **Configuration:** | **In-line four** |
| **Bhp:** | **270bhp** |
| **Max rpm:** | **8500rpm** |
| **Top speed:** | **160mph** |
| **0-60mph:** | **4sec** |
| **Weight:** | **1140kg** |
| **Gearbox:** | **H-pattern five-speed** |
| **Fuel:** | **Unleaded** |
| **Tyres:** | **Yokohama** |
| **Wheels:** | **17in rims** |
| **Front suspension:** | **Double joint McPherson strut with gas-filled dampers** |
| **Rear suspension:** | **Five-link multi-arm with gas-filled dampers** |
| **Brakes:** | **Iron discs front and rear** |

# Formula 1
# BMW Sauber F1.06

**First F1 chassis from BMW**

# Formula 1

# BMW Sauber F1.06

**First F1 chassis from BMW**

Frustrated by its perceived lack of success as an engine partner with Williams (2000–2005), BMW decided that Formula 1 success was best achieved by owning its own team. During 2005 it negotiated the take-over of Peter Sauber's Swiss-based team and ended its association with Williams. The short timescale of the deal meant that the 2006 car was a product of the ex-Sauber team led by technical boss Willy Rampf, explaining why the car retains the Sauber name in its title. The 2.4-litre V8 engine was designed and built in Munich, Germany, where BMW's head of motorsport, Mario Thiessen, is based. Former Sauber driver Nick Heidfeld followed BMW from Williams, while 1997 World Champion Jacques Villeneuve had a year remaining on his Sauber deal but was ejected from the team in mid-2006 and replaced by test driver Robert Kubica.

## Statistics

| | |
|---|---|
| **Chassis:** | **Carbon-fibre monocoque** |
| **Engine size:** | **2398cc** |
| **Configuration:** | **90-degree V8** |
| **Bhp:** | **750bhp** |
| **Max rpm:** | **19,000rpm** |
| **Top speed:** | **230mph** |
| **0-60mph:** | **2.1sec** |
| **Weight:** | **605kg (inc driver)** |
| **Gearbox:** | **Seven-speed semi-automatic** |
| **Fuel:** | **Petronas unleaded** |
| **Tyres:** | **Michelin** |
| **Wheels:** | **OZ** |
| **Front suspension:** | **Double wishbone mounted using 'zero-keel'** |
| **Rear suspension:** | **Double wishbone** |
| **Brakes:** | **Carbon-fibre discs front and rear** |

# FIA GT
## Chevrolet
## Corvette C6.R
**Americana shows Europeans the way in GT racing**

# FIA GT
# Chevrolet Corvette C6.R
**Americana shows Europeans the way in GT racing**

Chevrolet backed the development of the Corvette C6.R racer
to take on and beat the best of the European competition in
GT racing. Drawing on the experience of its successful C5-R
predecessor, the new car was launched ahead of the 2005
Sebring 12 Hours. While the C5 inspired the direction of the latest
car, the C6.R built upon this huge experience, and is General
Motors' most technologically advanced road-racing machine.
The racing version is shorter than its predecessor and lots of
work has been poured into making the C6.R as aerodynamically
efficient as possible. With its mammoth normally aspirated
7-litre engine, the car tops 180mph on Le Mans' famous
Mulsanne Straight and this was a key part of its stunning 2005
victory in the great race. A crack team of drivers, including three
ex-Formula 1 racers, have ensured the C6.R has continued to
enjoy a great level of success.

## Statistics

| | |
|---|---|
| Chassis: | Steel tubes with composite bodywork |
| Engine size: | 7000cc |
| Configuration: | Small-block V8 |
| Bhp: | 505bhp |
| Max rpm: | 7000rpm |
| Top speed: | 198mph |
| 0-60mph: | 3.9sec |
| Weight: | 1100kg |
| Gearbox: | Six-speed sequential |
| Fuel: | Mobil 1 unleaded |
| Tyres: | Michelin |
| Wheels: | 18in rims |
| Front suspension: | Double wishbone with adjustable dampers |
| Rear suspension: | Double wishbone with adjustable dampers |
| Brakes: | Carbon-fibre discs front and rear |

# WTCC
# Chevrolet Lacetti

**Uncle Sam goes far east man**

etandwin.com
andwin.com
Menu
CHEVROLET
CHEVROLET
CHEVROLE
KW suspension.de
GMAC
ADVAN
MAHLE

# Chevrolet Lacetti

**Uncle Sam goes far east man**

General Motors acquired Korean car manufacturer Daewoo in 1999. In 2005 GM decided to rebadge the Daewoos as Chevrolets and move its leading US brand into a growing global market. To increase awareness of Chevrolet's new status, GM entered the marque into the new World Touring Car Championship. Leading British engineering company Ray Mallock Limited was recruited to turn the ex-Daewoo Lacetti into a rival to BMW, SEAT and Alfa Romeo. It was an ambitious and well-funded project and star drivers Alain Menu and Nicola Larini, plus promising young Brit Rob Huff, were enticed on board. Initially the car struggled, but a rules break was allowed, permitting Chevrolet to incorporate parts of the Sodemo-built engine used by fellow GM brand Vauxhall in the British Touring Car Championship. The switch helped greatly and the bright blue cars have become regular top 10 contenders.

## Statistics

| | |
|---|---|
| **Chassis:** | **Tubular steel frame** |
| **Engine size:** | **1998cc** |
| **Configuration:** | **Four-cylinder in-line** |
| **Bhp:** | **270bhp** |
| **Max rpm:** | **8500rpm** |
| **Top speed:** | **155mph** |
| **0-60mph:** | **4.3sec** |
| **Weight:** | **1140kg inc driver** |
| **Gearbox:** | **Six-speed sequential** |
| **Fuel:** | **Unleaded** |
| **Tyres:** | **Dunlop** |
| **Wheels:** | **OZ 17in rims** |
| **Front suspension:** | **McPherson strut with coil springs** |
| **Rear suspension:** | **Dual-link rear axle with coil springs** |
| **Brakes:** | **Steel discs front and rear** |

# NASCAR
## Chevrolet Monte Carlo
**GM's veteran NASCAR racer**

# NASCAR
## Chevrolet
## Monte Carlo
**GM's veteran NASCAR racer**

General Motors is America's biggest car manufacturer and the Chevrolet Monte Carlo is its entry into America's biggest racing series – the NASCAR Nextel Cup. With both its main rivals, Dodge and Ford, introducing new models into the series over the past two seasons, Chevrolet brought in the new Monte Carlo SS for 2006. It had a lot to live up to as its predecessor stole the 2005 title in the hands of Tony Stewart. Top-notch outfits like Hendrick Motorsports, Joe Gibbs Racing and Dale Earnhardt Inc. have kept the Monte Carlo at the head of the field, with stars like four-time champion Jeff Gordon and his protégé Jimmie Johnson behind the wheel. Chevrolet offers a road version of the SS, although with considerably less horsepower than the 700-plus the NASCAR small-block V8 racing car produces.

## Statistics

| | |
|---|---|
| **Chassis:** | **Tubular steel frame** |
| **Engine size:** | **5866cc** |
| **Configuration:** | **V8** |
| **Bhp:** | **850bhp** |
| **Max rpm:** | **9000rpm** |
| **Top speed:** | **199mph** |
| **0-60mph:** | **4.0sec** |
| **Weight:** | **1542kg** |
| **Gearbox:** | **Four-speed manual** |
| **Fuel:** | **Sunoco 112 octane** |
| **Tyres:** | **Goodyear** |
| **Wheels:** | **15in rims** |
| **Front suspension:** | **Twin control arms, independent coil springs** |
| **Rear suspension:** | **Trailing arms and coil springs** |
| **Brakes:** | **Steel discs front and rear** |

# IRL
# Dallara-Honda

**The fastest racing series in the world**

# IRL
# Dallara-Honda

**The fastest racing series in the world**

In 1996 Tony George, the owner of the Indianapolis 500 – the world's richest race – started his own race series, the Indy Racing League. Over the past decade it has been rebranded as IRL IndyCar and attracted many of North America's leading single-seater teams and drivers. Dallara and Panoz won the right to supply cars to the series, but for 2006 all bar the Rahal-Letterman team opted for the Dallara version. With the series made up of 14 races, 11 of which are held on ovals where speeds top 220mph, the IRL can claim to be the fastest single-seater series in the world. Because of this, the cars have to be exceptionally strong. The cars are technically low-spec, with no traction control and stick shift sequential gearboxes. The Honda engine is a 3-litre V8 run on alcohol and produces around 700bhp.

## Statistics

| | |
|---|---|
| **Chassis:** | **Carbon-fibre composite** |
| **Engine size:** | **3000cc** |
| **Configuration:** | **V8** |
| **Bhp:** | **700bhp** |
| **Max rpm:** | **10,000rpm** |
| **Top speed:** | **235mph** |
| **0-60mph:** | **2.3sec** |
| **Weight:** | **691kg** |
| **Gearbox:** | **Six-speed sequential** |
| **Fuel:** | **Ethanol/methanol blend** |
| **Tyres:** | **Firestone** |
| **Wheels:** | **15in rims** |
| **Front suspension:** | **Double wishbone with pushrod-activated torsion springs** |
| **Rear suspension:** | **Double wishbone with pushrod-activated torsion springs** |
| **Brakes:** | **Carbon-fibre discs front and rear** |

# Formula 3
# Dallara-Mercedes F306

**Building on 10 years of unrivalled success**

# Formula 3
# Dallara-Mercedes F306

**Building on 10 years of unrivalled success**

For the past decade, Italian chassis constructor Dallara has ruled the roost in Formula 3. Its cars have taken all the major titles from South America to Japan, but it's in the key European markets where its success has been most telling. With top outfits like ASM, Manor Motorsport and Carlin Motorsport pushing their own development programmes alongside Dallara's in-house effort, the Italian cars have been practically unbeatable, especially in the high-profile Euroseries, where Mercedes-powered versions have swept to the past two titles. The HWA-built 2-litre engine is one of the most powerful F3 units and it's also the lightest and most compact. This has allowed the teams to maximise the efficiency of its installation to create lower centres of gravity and produce even sweeter handling cars. In the hands of drivers like Lewis Hamilton, Jamie Green and Bruno Senna, this has been rewarded with repeated high levels of success.

## Statistics

| | |
|---|---|
| **Chassis:** | **Carbon-fibre monocoque** |
| **Engine size:** | **1997cc** |
| **Configuration:** | **In-line four** |
| **Bhp:** | **210bhp** |
| **Max rpm:** | **6000rpm** |
| **Top speed:** | **160mph** |
| **0-60mph:** | **3.0sec** |
| **Weight:** | **550kg (inc driver)** |
| **Gearbox:** | **Six-speed sequential** |
| **Fuel:** | **Unleaded** |
| **Tyres:** | **Kumho (Euroseries)** |
| **Wheels:** | **ATS 13in rims** |
| **Front suspension:** | **Double wishbone with a choice of damper specifications** |
| **Rear suspension:** | **Double wishbone with pushrods** |
| **Brakes:** | **Carbon-fibre discs front and rear** |

# GP2
# Dallara-Renault
**The last step before Formula 1**

# GP2
# Dallara-Renault

**The last step before Formula 1**

GP2 was launched in 2005 with the aim of creating the final rung on the ladder to racing in Formula 1. Italian engineering specialist Dallara was commissioned to design the chassis and produced a sturdy, aerodynamically sophisticated monocoque, which is mated to a Renault-badged 4-litre V8 engine pumping out 600bhp. For its first season the GP2 category used F1-style grooved tyres and this created action-packed close racing, with overtaking commonplace throughout the field. For 2006 tyres were changed in favour of Bridgestone slicks, but the entertainment factor hasn't been dimmed. The extra grip means GP2 cars are now only around 10 seconds per lap slower than the fastest F1 cars. This makes the series a great feeder formula and it has already taken 2005 champion Nico Rosberg, Heikki Kovalainen, Scott Speed, Neel Jani and Giorgio Mondini into F1 test and race roles.

## Statistics

| | |
|---|---|
| **Chassis:** | **Carbon-fibre monocoque with aluminium honeycomb** |
| **Engine size:** | **4000cc** |
| **Configuration:** | **V8** |
| **Bhp:** | **600bhp** |
| **Max rpm:** | **10,000rpm** |
| **Top speed:** | **201mph** |
| **0-60mph:** | **2.9sec** |
| **Weight:** | **667kg (inc driver)** |
| **Gearbox:** | **Six-speed semi-automatic sequential gearbox** |
| **Fuel:** | **Unleaded** |
| **Tyres:** | **Bridgestone slicks** |
| **Wheels:** | **OZ front: 13in x 12in, rear: 13in x 13.7in** |
| **Front suspension:** | **Double wishbone, pushrods, twin dampers** |
| **Rear suspension:** | **Double wishbone, pushrods, twin dampers** |
| **Brakes:** | **Carbon-fibre discs front and rear** |

# World Series
# Dallara-Renault
**Europe's second fastest single-seater series**

EUROINTER

# World Series
# Dallara-Renault

**Europe's second fastest single-seater series**

The World Series by Renault is a fast single-spec series that slots in between GP2 and Formula 3 on the single-seater ladder. The series was the result of combining the World Series by Nissan and the Renault V6 Eurocup championship at the end of 2004, after Renault took a controlling stake in Nissan. The Dallara chassis is an evolution of the Nissan car. Its wide track and ground-effect aerodynamics make it a very high-grip car capable of cornering speeds approaching those in Formula 1. The Solution F-built 3.5-litre Renault engine produces 425bhp and the sticky Michelin slick tyres combine to create a very fast car that requires total commitment from its drivers. The series has been very well supported, with bumper grids of 30 cars. The series champion gets a test in the Renault F1 car, and 2005 title winner Robert Kubica's performance in this helped him to secure the test driver role at BMW Sauber.

## Statistics

| | |
|---|---|
| Chassis: | Carbon-fibre monocoque |
| Engine size: | 3498cc |
| Configuration: | V6 |
| Bhp: | 425bhp |
| Max rpm: | 8500rpm |
| Top speed: | 180mph |
| 0-60mph: | 2.6sec |
| Weight: | 600kg |
| Gearbox: | Six-speed sequential with paddle shift |
| Fuel: | Unleaded |
| Tyres: | Michelin |
| Wheels: | OZ 13in rims |
| Front suspension: | Double wishbone with adjustable dampers |
| Rear suspension: | Double wishbone with adjustable dampers |
| Brakes: | Carbon-fibre discs front and rear |

# Grand Am
# Daytona Prototype

**NASCAR goes sportscar racing**

# Grand Am
# Daytona Prototype
**NASCAR goes sportscar racing**

After enjoying considerable success in the 1970s and '80s, by the mid-'90s sportscar racing was almost dead in the United States. Enter the France family of NASCAR fame, which established the Grand American Road Racing Association in 1999. For 2003 it launched the Daytona Prototype class, opened the formula up to a variety of chassis and engine suppliers, and found itself with a massive hit on its hands. Seven approved constructors – Riley, Doran, Crawford, Fabcar, Chase, Picchio and Multimatic – supply the cars, while Pontiac (5-litre V8), Lexus (4.3-litre V8), BMW (5-litre V8), Porsche (3.9-litre flat-six), Ford (5-litre V8) and Infiniti (4.3-litre V8) provide the power. The vast number of chassis-engine combinations, plus entries from leading road racing teams such as Ganassi Racing, has made the Grand Am series one of the most competitive in the world, with close, hard-fought races.

## Statistics

| | |
|---|---|
| **Chassis:** | **Tubular steel frame with composite bodywork** |
| **Engine size:** | **Cat 1 up to 4000cc Cat 2 up to 5000cc** |
| **Layout:** | **Cat 1: six or eight cylinders, Cat 2: V8** |
| **Bhp:** | **500bhp** |
| **Max rpm:** | **8100rpm** |
| **Top speed:** | **210mph** |
| **0-60mph:** | **4sec** |
| **Weight:** | **Up to 3.99L 975kg, 4.0 to 4.5L 998kg, 4.51 to 5.0L 1032kg** |
| **Gearbox:** | **Five- or six-speed sequential** |
| **Fuel:** | **Unleaded** |
| **Tyres:** | **Hoosier** |
| **Wheels:** | **14in rims** |
| **Front suspension:** | **Double wishbone single spring per wheel** |
| **Rear suspension:** | **Double wishbone single spring per wheel** |
| **Brakes:** | **Carbon-fibre discs front and rear** |

# NASCAR
# Dodge Charger

**Iconic muscle back on track**

# Dodge Charger

**Iconic muscle back on track**

Dodge is the brand DaimlerChrysler promotes in NASCAR, America's biggest form of motorsport. The Charger model was introduced in 2005, when it replaced the long-serving Intrepid. The Charger name is one of the most evocative in American muscle car history, due in part to the car's starring role in the 1970s cult road movie *Vanishing Point*. The current Charger aims to recreate the spirit of that age and the stock car racing version is a key element of this. With two of NASCAR's strongest outfits, Team Penske and Bill Davis Racing, running the Charger, it has already entered the winners' circle, and it will need to do that regularly if it's to end Dodge's championship win drought dating back to 1975, when stock car legend Richard Petty took the second of his back-to-back titles in the STP-liveried Charger.

## Statistics

| | |
|---|---|
| **Chassis:** | **Tubular steel frame** |
| **Engine size:** | **5866cc** |
| **Configuration:** | **V8** |
| **Bhp:** | **850bhp** |
| **Max rpm:** | **9000rpm** |
| **Top speed:** | **200mph** |
| **0-60mph:** | **4.0sec** |
| **Weight:** | **1542kg** |
| **Gearbox:** | **Four-speed manual** |
| **Fuel:** | **Sunoco 112 octane** |
| **Tyres:** | **Goodyear** |
| **Wheels:** | **15in rims** |
| **Front suspension:** | **Independent double A arms** |
| **Rear suspension:** | **Floating live axle on trailing arms** |
| **Brakes:** | **Carbon-fibre discs front and rear** |

# Formula 1
# Ferrari F248

**Keeping the legend alive**

# Formula 1
# Ferrari F248

**Keeping the legend alive**

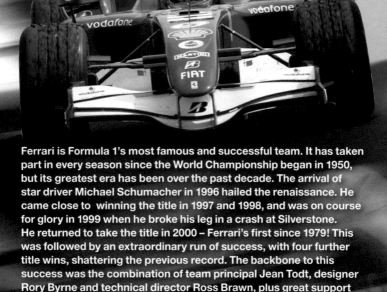

Ferrari is Formula 1's most famous and successful team. It has taken part in every season since the World Championship began in 1950, but its greatest era has been over the past decade. The arrival of star driver Michael Schumacher in 1996 hailed the renaissance. He came close to winning the title in 1997 and 1998, and was on course for glory in 1999 when he broke his leg in a crash at Silverstone. He returned to take the title in 2000 – Ferrari's first since 1979! This was followed by an extraordinary run of success, with four further title wins, shattering the previous record. The backbone to this success was the combination of team principal Jean Todt, designer Rory Byrne and technical director Ross Brawn, plus great support from Bridgestone tyres. Byrne is now semi-retired and the F248 is the work of designer Aldo Costa. In their traditional red livery, the Ferraris of Schumacher and new team-mate Felipe Massa are the best-supported cars on the grid, with thousands of fans turning out to cheer their favourites home at each race.

## Statistics

| | |
|---|---|
| **Chassis:** | **Carbon-fibre monocoque** |
| **Engine size:** | **2398cc** |
| **Configuration:** | **V8** |
| **Bhp:** | **760bhp** |
| **Max rpm:** | **19,500rpm** |
| **Top speed:** | **231mph** |
| **0-60mph:** | **2.1sec** |
| **Weight:** | **605kg (inc driver)** |
| **Gearbox:** | **Seven-speed semi-automatic** |
| **Fuel:** | **Shell unleaded** |
| **Tyres:** | **Bridgestone** |
| **Wheels:** | **13in rims** |
| **Front suspension:** | **Double wishbone with pushrods** |
| **Rear suspension:** | **Double wishbone with pushrods** |
| **Brakes:** | **Carbon-fibre discs front and rear** |

# V8 Supercars
# Ford Falcon

**Flame-spitting monster from down-under**

# V8 Supercars
# Ford Falcon

**Flame-spitting monster from down-under**

The V8 Supercar championship is Australia's most popular and successful form of motorsport, with huge crowds drawn to watch the spectacular racing. Ford and arch-rival Holden have supported the series since its rebirth in 1993. In that time Ford has remained loyal to its Falcon model, although it has undergone a series of revisions over the years – the current version is the BA. Although Ford officially backs a number of teams, the cars and engines are developed by the teams themselves. With 5-litre V8 engines, power outputs reach an impressive 635bhp, making these rear-wheel-drive beasts hard to tame. The rivalry between Ford and Holden is fierce, but in recent years the Blue Oval has held the upper hand, winning the past three titles with Marcos Ambrose and Russell Ingall. Prodrive-run Ford Performance Racing, Stone Brothers Racing and Triple Eight Racing are among the top Falcon campaigners.

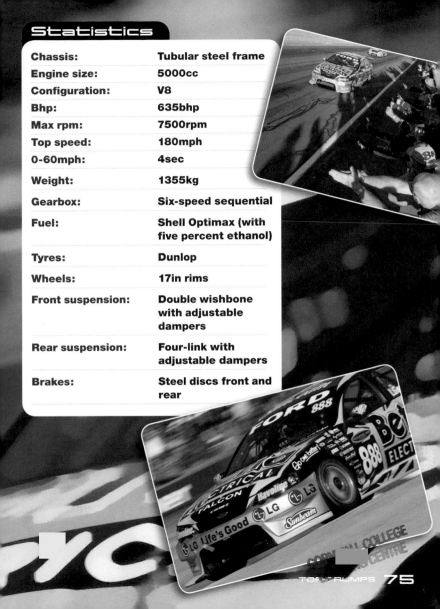

## Statistics

| | |
|---|---|
| Chassis: | Tubular steel frame |
| Engine size: | 5000cc |
| Configuration: | V8 |
| Bhp: | 635bhp |
| Max rpm: | 7500rpm |
| Top speed: | 180mph |
| 0-60mph: | 4sec |
| Weight: | 1355kg |
| Gearbox: | Six-speed sequential |
| Fuel: | Shell Optimax (with five percent ethanol) |
| Tyres: | Dunlop |
| Wheels: | 17in rims |
| Front suspension: | Double wishbone with adjustable dampers |
| Rear suspension: | Four-link with adjustable dampers |
| Brakes: | Steel discs front and rear |

# NASCAR
# Ford Fusion

**New look for Ford's NASCAR challenger**

# NASCAR
# Ford Fusion

**New look for Ford's NASCAR challenger**

For the first time since 1968, Ford simultaneously launched a new road car model and NASCAR challenger in 2006. That car was the Fusion, which replaced the venerable Taurus. The Fusion is a much more modern-looking machine than its predecessor, which had raced in different guises for 20 years. And the Fusion soon took over the Taurus's winning mantle to become Ford's seventh different model to win in NASCAR's premier stock car series. With the crack Roush Racing outfit overseeing the leading Fusion entries, Ford has an elite list of drivers in its camp including veteran Mark Martin, rising stars Greg Biffle and Carl Edwards, and former champion Matt Kenseth, who claimed the title in 2003. As well as chassis development, Roush also build and supply the 5.9-litre V8 engines to most of the other Ford entrants in the series.

| | |
|---|---|
| **Chassis:** | **Tubular steel frame** |
| **Engine size:** | **5866cc** |
| **Configuration:** | **V8** |
| **Bhp:** | **850bhp** |
| **Max rpm:** | **9000rpm** |
| **Top speed:** | **199mph** |
| **0-60mph:** | **4.0sec** |
| **Weight:** | **1542kg** |
| **Gearbox:** | **Four-speed manual** |
| **Fuel:** | **Sunoco 112 octane** |
| **Tyres:** | **Goodyear** |
| **Wheels:** | **15in rims** |
| **Front suspension:** | **Twin control arms, independent coil springs** |
| **Rear suspension:** | **Trailing arms and coil springs** |
| **Brakes:** | **Carbon-fibre discs front and rear** |

# Grand Prix
# Masters

**A 200mph racer for ex-F1 stars**

# Grand Prix
# Masters

**A 200mph racer for ex-F1 stars**

The Grand Prix Masters was created to replicate in the motor racing sphere the success of the seniors tours in golf and tennis. British-based engineering company Delta Motorsport was hired to construct 16 equal single-seater cars, which are based on the Reynard Champ Car of 1999 vintage, but have been substantially overhauled and reinforced to ensure that the veteran drivers – all competitors have to be over 45 – are as safe as possible. Power comes from a 3.5-litre Nicholson McLaren engine based on the highly-successful Cosworth XB unit. It has had its turbo removed and been detuned to around 600bhp for maximum reliability. All technical data is freely available to all the drivers to ensure the cars are fairly matched. Former World Champions Nigel Mansell and Emerson Fittipaldi were among the star names to attend the first Masters race at Kyalami, South Africa, in 2005. Always a fierce competitor, Mansell won that debut race and also the first 2006 event in Qatar.

## Statistics

| | |
|---|---|
| **Chassis:** | **Carbon-fibre monocoque** |
| **Engine size:** | **3500cc** |
| **Configuration:** | **80-degree V8** |
| **Bhp:** | **600bhp** |
| **Max rpm:** | **10,400rpm** |
| **Top speed:** | **200mph** |
| **0-60mph:** | **2.6sec** |
| **Weight:** | **650kg** |
| **Gearbox:** | **Six-speed semi-automatic** |
| **Fuel:** | **Unleaded** |
| **Tyres:** | **Avon** |
| **Wheels:** | **14in rims** |
| **Front suspension:** | **Double wishbone with pushrods** |
| **Rear suspension:** | **Double wishbone with pushrods** |
| **Brakes:** | **Iron discs front and rear with carbon-fibre pads** |

# V8 Supercars
# Holden Commodore

**This one doesn't take it easy like Sunday morning**

# V8 Supercars
# Holden Commodore

**This one doesn't take it easy like Sunday morning**

Like Ford and its Falcon, GM-owned Holden has kept faith with the Commodore model for its V8 Supercar challenge, and in 2006 the flame-spitting 5-litre monster ran in the latest VZ specification. The two marques divide opinion among Supercar fans, with the Aussies remaining steadfastly loyal to their preferred brand, and driver switches across marques causing uproar. In 2006 the regulations were revised slightly, with reverse grids introduced for the third race (of three) on the weekend. This created even more action as drivers are forced to fight for position on the tight Aussie tracks in wide and heavy cars, the result being plenty of crowd-pleasing crashes. The Holden Racing Team, with drivers Mark Skaife and Todd Kelly, is the top Commodore outfit. Skaife was Holden's last title winner, his 2002 triumph being his third in a row and his fifth in total.

## Statistics

| | |
|---|---|
| **Chassis:** | **Tubular steel frame** |
| **Engine size:** | **5000cc** |
| **Configuration:** | **V8** |
| **Bhp:** | **635bhp** |
| **Max rpm:** | **7500rpm** |
| **Top speed:** | **180mph** |
| **0-60mph:** | **4sec** |
| **Weight:** | **1355kg** |
| **Gearbox:** | **Six-speed sequential** |
| **Fuel:** | **Mobil unleaded** |
| **Tyres:** | **Dunlop** |
| **Wheels:** | **OZ 11in rim** |
| **Front suspension:** | **Double wishbone with adjustable dampers** |
| **Rear suspension:** | **Four-link parallel arms with adjustable dampers** |
| **Brakes:** | **Steel discs front and rear** |

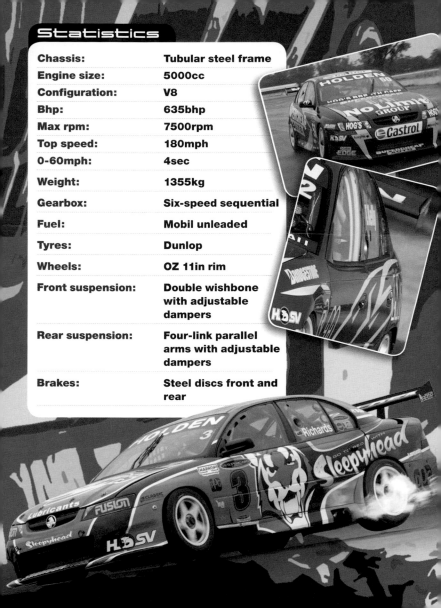

# BTCC
# Honda Integra-R

**Independents show the future's orange**

# BTCC
# Honda Integra-R

**Independents show the future's orange**

Team Dynamics struck a blow for independent touring car teams in 2005 when it claimed the British Touring Car Championship with its in-house developed Honda Integra Type-R. The Integra is an oddball in the series, given that the car is not officially available in the UK. However, the stunning performance of the road-going version means there's a healthy number of 'grey imports' seen on British roads. In spite of this, Dynamics boss Steve Neal was convinced of the potential of a BTCC Integra, and for 2005 his team produced three cars with power coming courtesy of Honda engine specialist Neil Brown. The package was an instant hit. The car's slippery shape made it fast in a straight line, while the well-balanced chassis used its tyres sparingly, meaning it was always strong late in races, even when fully laden with success ballast. In Matt Neal's hands it claimed the title and is favourite for a repeat in 2006.

## Statistics

| | |
|---|---|
| **Chassis:** | **Tubular steel frame** |
| **Engine size:** | **2000cc** |
| **Configuration:** | **In-line four** |
| **Bhp:** | **300bhp** |
| **Max rpm:** | **9000rpm** |
| **Top speed:** | **150mph** |
| **0-60mph:** | **4.8sec** |
| **Weight:** | **1150kg (inc driver)** |
| **Gearbox:** | **Six-speed sequential** |
| **Fuel:** | **Unleaded** |
| **Tyres:** | **Dunlop** |
| **Wheels:** | **17in rims** |
| **Front suspension:** | **McPherson strut with three-way adjustable damper** |
| **Rear suspension:** | **Single wishbone with three-way adjustable damper** |

# Super GT
# Honda NSX

**Venerable racer still taking wins**

# Super GT
# Honda NSX

**Venerable racer still taking wins**

The Honda NSX may be Honda's longest-serving road model, but that hasn't stopped it remaining a formidable force in Super GT racing. Not that the NSX used in Japan's domestic sportscar series has much in common with the road-going model. Super GT rules insist that a car retain the same shape body panels and dimensions as the original, but allows the use of lightweight composites, a host of downforce-producing aerodynamic wings and flaps, and modifications to the engine including turbo- and super-charging. These all combine to create an exotic-looking grid in which the NSX, with its distinctive overhead air intake, looks right at home. Chassis specialists Dome have race-tuned the NSX's chassis, while power comes from an M-Tec-developed 3-litre V6 twin-turbo powerplant. Team Honda Racing and Nakajima Racing are Honda's leading entrants as it seeks its first title win since Ryo Michigami in 2000.

## Statistics

| | |
|---|---|
| **Chassis:** | Tubular steel frame |
| **Engine size:** | 3464cc |
| **Configuration:** | 60-degree V6 twin-turbo |
| **Bhp:** | 500bhp |
| **Max rpm:** | 7000rpm |
| **Top speed:** | 190mph |
| **0-60mph:** | 3.9sec |
| **Weight:** | 1100kg |
| **Gearbox:** | Six-speed sequential |
| **Fuel:** | 102 Ron unleaded |
| **Tyres:** | Bridgestone |
| **Wheels:** | 13in rims |
| **Front suspension:** | Double wishbone with pushrods |
| **Rear suspension:** | Double wishbone with pushrods |
| **Brakes:** | Steel discs front and rear |

# Formula 1
# Honda RA106

**Honda raises the bar with team takeover**

# Formula 1
# Honda RA106

**Honda raises the bar with team takeover**

Between the end of the 2005 season and the start of 2006, Japanese car giant Honda completed the takeover of the BAR team, thus creating its first fully-owned Formula 1 team since 1968. Honda had supplied BAR with engines since 2000 and achieved considerable success in 2004 when the combination finished second in the championship. However, a win proved elusive and the decision was taken that ultimate glory could only be achieved by taking control of the whole operation. The project remains based in Banbury in the UK, where technical director Geoff Willis oversees the design and construction of the car. The 2.4-litre V8 engines are shipped in from Japan and the team has been a long-term user of Michelin tyres. Jenson Button, who finally won his first GP in Hungary in 2006, is partnered by Rubens Barrichello, who had six seasons alongside Michael Schumacher at Ferrari.

# Statistics

| | |
|---|---|
| **Chassis:** | **Carbon-fibre composite** |
| **Engine size:** | **2400cc** |
| **Configuration:** | **V8** |
| **Bhp:** | **750bhp** |
| **Max rpm:** | **19,250rpm** |
| **Top speed:** | **230mph** |
| **0-60mph:** | **2.1sec** |
| **Weight:** | **605kg (inc driver)** |
| **Gearbox:** | **Seven-speed semi-automatic** |
| **Fuel:** | **Unleaded** |
| **Tyres:** | **Michelin** |
| **Wheels:** | **BBS 13in rims** |
| **Front suspension:** | **Double wishbone with pushrod-activated torsion springs** |
| **Rear suspension:** | **Double wishbone with pushrod-activated torsion springs** |
| **Brakes:** | **Carbon-fibre discs front and rear** |

# FIA GT
# Lamborghini
# Murciélago R-GT
**Raging bull of the international GT scene**

For a company so famous for making high-performance supercars,
Lamborghini has a surprisingly limited and unsuccessful heritage
in motor racing. Incredibly, 2006 was the first time that the Italian
marque appeared in the Le Mans 24 Hours. The car entered
was the fabulous-looking Murciélago. The car is run by the
German Reiter Engineering team, which specialises in producing
aftermarket parts for road-going Lambos and receives some
support from Lamborghini, although it's by no means a full works
effort. The race version runs in the highly competitive FIA GT
championship, where it's eligible for the GT1 class. This means the
car, while outwardly similar to showroom Murciélagos, is a pure-
bred racer, with sophisticated suspension made from lightweight
composites, while a 6-litre V12 engine provides the grunt that
allows the car to hit almost 200mph along the awesome Mulsanne
Straight at Le Mans.

## Statistics

| | |
|---|---|
| **Chassis:** | **Carbon-fibre monocoque** |
| **Engine size:** | **5998cc** |
| **Configuration:** | **60-degree V12** |
| **Bhp:** | **620bhp** |
| **Max rpm:** | **6100rpm** |
| **Top speed:** | **196mph** |
| **0-60mph:** | **3.9sec** |
| **Weight:** | **1100kg (in FIA GT)** |
| **Gearbox:** | **Six-speed sequential** |
| **Fuel:** | **Unleaded** |
| **Tyres:** | **Michelin** |
| **Wheels:** | **15in rims** |
| **Front suspension:** | **Double wishbone with pushrods** |
| **Rear suspension:** | **Double wishbone with pushrods** |
| **Brakes:** | **Carbon-fibre discs front and rear** |

# Super GT
# Lexus SC430

**Toyota takes luxury brand into racing**

# Super GT
# Lexus SC430

**Toyota takes luxury brand into racing**

With its Supra model out-dated and no longer on sale, Toyota needed a new model to race in the highly successful Japanese Super GT series. With its Lexus brand on the up, and no natural successor to the Supra in its own model line-up, Toyota decided to endorse the first works-supported Lexus race programme. The car chosen was the sports coupé, the SC430, and four cars were prepared for the start of the season and entrusted to the best-placed Supra-running teams from 2005. Despite rumours over the winter that the Lexus was no match for the car it replaced, it made a sensational debut, winning first time out at Suzuka. Long-time Toyota runners TOM's, Team Le Mans, Team Kraft and defending champions Team Cerumo race the cars, which retain the 4.5-litre normally-aspirated engine used so successfully in the Supra.

## Statistics

| | |
|---|---|
| **Chassis:** | Steel tubular frame |
| **Engine size:** | 4480cc |
| **Configuration:** | V8 |
| **Bhp:** | 480bhp |
| **Max rpm:** | 7200rpm |
| **Top speed:** | 180mph |
| **0-60mph:** | 3.3sec |
| **Weight:** | 1100kg |
| **Gearbox:** | Six-speed sequential |
| **Fuel:** | Unleaded |
| **Tyres:** | Bridgestone/Dunlop |
| **Wheels:** | 18in rims |
| **Front suspension:** | Double wishbone |
| **Rear suspension:** | Double wishbone |
| **Brakes:** | Steel discs front and rear |

# Champ Car
# Lola-Ford

**Final hurrah for Lola's old warhorse**

# Champ Car
# Lola-Ford

**Final hurrah for Lola's old warhorse**

The Lola-Ford Champ Car is the old stager of the single-seater world. Originally introduced for the 2000 season as the B2K/00, the car has been kept in service as Champ Car needed a low-cost, reliable chassis platform after its near financial collapse and subsequent relaunching for 2004. However, 2006 is the final year for the old warhorse, and an all-new Panoz-built chassis is being introduced in 2007. The Lola has undergone a subtle and controlled development over the past six years. The car is strong, as is required for racing on ovals, and quite heavy as a result. With no electronic gizmos such as semi-automatic gearboxes or traction control, it's a challenge to drive. The Cosworth-built Ford engine has been around even longer than the chassis. In pre-2004-spec, it used to pump out almost 900bhp, but since the series became a single engine formula it has been detuned for reliability and now produces around 750bhp plus a 30bhp 'push to pass' booster.

## Statistics

| | |
|---|---|
| **Chassis:** | **Carbon-fibre monocoque** |
| **Engine size:** | **2650cc** |
| **Configuration:** | **Turbo-charged V8** |
| **Bhp:** | **750bhp** |
| **Max rpm:** | **16,000rpm** |
| **Top speed:** | **240mph** |
| **0-60mph:** | **2.2sec** |
| **Weight:** | **709kg** |
| **Gearbox:** | **Seven-speed sequential** |
| **Fuel:** | **Methanol** |
| **Tyres:** | **Bridgestone** |
| **Wheels:** | **OZ 14in rim** |
| **Front suspension:** | **Double wishbone with inboard dampers** |
| **Rear suspension:** | **Double wishbone with inboard dampers** |
| **Brakes:** | **Cast iron discs front and rear (carbon-fibre discs permitted at some circuits)** |

# Forumla Nippon
# Lola FN06

**Japan rises to the challenge of GP2**

# Forumla Nippon
# Lola FN06

**Japan rises to the challenge of GP2**

Formula Nippon is Japan's top single-seater series. For 2006 the championship commissioned Lola to produce a new chassis to accommodate ex-IRL IndyCar engines from Honda and Toyota. With support from two of Japan's biggest motor manufacturers, the series has once again attracted top European drivers as it used to do in the 1990s, when future F1 aces such as Eddie Irvine, Heinz-Harald Frentzen and Ralf Schumacher raced in the Far East. The change of engine to 4-litre V8s has boosted power to around 600bhp, making the series a direct rival to the Europe-based GP2 championship. The cars are around 1.5 seconds faster than the ones they replaced and with races lasting over an hour and held in often gruelling conditions in the heat of the Japanese summer, Formula Nippon offers a physical challenge that's ideal for preparing drivers for a future step into F1.

| | |
|---|---|
| **Chassis:** | **Carbon-fibre skin over aluminium honeycomb core** |
| **Engine size:** | **3000cc** |
| **Configuration:** | **V8** |
| **Bhp:** | **550bhp** |
| **Max rpm:** | **10,000rpm** |
| **Top speed:** | **185mph** |
| **0-60mph:** | **2.6sec** |
| **Weight:** | **590kg** |
| **Gearbox:** | **Six-speed sequential** |
| **Fuel:** | **Unleaded** |
| **Tyres:** | **Bridgestone** |
| **Wheels:** | **OZ 13in rims** |
| **Front suspension:** | **Double wishbone with pushrods** |
| **Rear suspension:** | **Double wishbone with pushrods** |
| **Brakes:** | **Carbon-fibre discs front and rear** |

# Formula 3
# Lola–Mugen B06/30

**British challenge to Italian domination**

# Formula 3
# Lola-Mugen B06/30

**British challenge to Italian domination**

Lola has been the main challenger to Dallara's position of
dominance in the Formula 3 market. Its B06/30 is a development
of the chassis it produced in conjunction with Japanese chassis
specialist Dome. The result was a distinctive car that was at its
best in fast sweeping corners where it was able to exploit its aero
efficiency. This delivered wins at the high-speed Thruxton circuit
in the British F3 Championship in 2004 and at Castle Combe in
2005. But with economies of scale always favouring the numerical
advantage of the Dallaras, Lola was unable to persuade a top
team to enter into partnership and develop the car, so for 2006
it has taken its challenge to the lower-profile German-based F3
Recaro Cup, where it has been a regular race winner. In the hands
of Cornishman Joey Foster, the Opel-powered Lola was a genuine
title challenger, but Foster was injured in a heavy mid-season crash
and forced to sit out the remainder of the championship.

## Statistics

| | |
|---|---|
| **Chassis:** | **Carbon-fibre skin over aluminium honeycomb core** |
| **Engine size:** | **1998cc** |
| **Configuration:** | **In-line four** |
| **Bhp:** | **207bhp** |
| **Max rpm:** | **6000rpm** |
| **Top speed:** | **160mph** |
| **0-60mph:** | **3.0sec** |
| **Weight:** | **550kg (inc driver)** |
| **Gearbox:** | **Six-speed sequential** |
| **Fuel:** | **Unleaded** |
| **Tyres:** | **Avon** |
| **Wheels:** | **13in rims** |
| **Front suspension:** | **Double wishbone with pushrods** |
| **Rear suspension:** | **Double wishbone with pushrods** |
| **Brakes:** | **Carbon-fibre discs front and rear** |

A1 Grand Prix
# Lola-Zytek
**Uniting the world through racing**

# A1 Grand Prix
# Lola-Zytek

**Uniting the world through racing**

A1 Grand Prix is a unique motorsport concept that pitches country against country, rather than driver against driver. Launched in 2005, the series is the brainchild of Sheikh Maktoum of Dubai. The concept was a success, attracting established motorsport nations such as Great Britain and France as well as places without racing heritage such as Lebanon and Pakistan. Lola won the tender to build the chassis and it produced a very strong car based around its venerable Formula 3000 design fitted with some outlandish bodywork. Zytek was commissioned to build the engine and adapted its 4-litre V8 sportscar engine for the series. The package worked well and on huge Cooper slick tyres the cars produced spectator-friendly slides and great racing and overtaking, helped in part by a 30bhp 'boost button'. The cars withstood some huge crashes too, and amazingly there wasn't a single engine failure over the whole of the series, which ran over the winter of 2005/06 visiting places such as Dubai, Australia and Mexico.

## Statistics

| | |
|---|---|
| **Chassis:** | **Aluminium honeycomb with carbon skin** |
| **Engine size:** | **3400cc** |
| **Configuration:** | **90-degree V8** |
| **Bhp:** | **520bhp** |
| **Max rpm:** | **9000rpm** |
| **Top speed:** | **195mph** |
| **0-60mph:** | **2.9sec** |
| **Weight:** | **600kg** |
| **Gearbox:** | **Six-speed sequential with paddle shift** |
| **Fuel:** | **100 RON unleaded** |
| **Tyres:** | **Cooper** |
| **Wheels:** | **13in rims** |
| **Front suspension:** | **Double wishbone with pushrods** |
| **Rear suspension:** | **Double wishbone with pushrods** |
| **Brakes:** | **Steel discs with carbon pads** |

# FIA GT
# Maserati MC12

**The ultimate supercar racer**

# FIA GT
# Maserati MC12

**The ultimate supercar racer**

The Maserati MC12 is the car that took Maserati back into
international sportscar racing for the first time in almost 40 years.
The striking-looking machine is based on the Ferrari Enzo and
a handful of road-going versions were built to ensure the car's
eligibility for the FIA GT series. Such was the amazing performance
of the MC12 that when it arrived on the scene in 2005, it raised
the performance bar considerably. This led to calls for its pace to
be capped, and the MC12 literally had its wings clipped and was
forced to run to revised aerodynamic regulations. With these in
place, the car was granted a special invitation into the American Le
Mans Series. Despite this, the MC12's width has precluded it from
gaining a place on the grid for the Le Mans 24 Hours. Nevertheless,
in GT racing the MC12, in the hands of the works-backed Vitaphone
team, remains a highly competitive racer.

| | |
|---|---|
| **Chassis:** | **Carbon-fibre monocoque with aluminium sub-chassis** |
| **Engine size:** | **5998cc** |
| **Configuration:** | **65-degree V12** |
| **Bhp:** | **630bhp** |
| **Max rpm:** | **7700rpm** |
| **Top speed:** | **205mph** |
| **0-60mph:** | **3.8sec** |
| **Weight:** | **1335kg** |
| **Gearbox:** | **Six-speed sequential** |
| **Fuel:** | **Unleaded** |
| **Tyres:** | **Michelin** |
| **Wheels:** | **19in rims** |
| **Front suspension:** | **Double wishbone with pushrods** |
| **Rear suspension:** | **Double wishbone with pushrods** |
| **Brakes:** | **Carbon-fibre discs front and rear** |

# Formula 1
# McLaren MP4-21

**Silver dream machine**

# Formula 1
# McLaren MP4-21

**Silver dream machine**

McLaren celebrated its 40th year in Formula 1 in 2006, and the team founded by New Zealander Bruce McLaren remains one of the sport's most accomplished outfits. The 2006 car, the MP4-21, was arguably the most striking on the grid, with its metallic chrome paint scheme and ultra-compact aerodynamic package. It's also the first McLaren since 1997 to have been developed without the presence of star aerodynamicist Adrian Newey, who oversaw the car's design but joined Red Bull Racing at the end of 2005. Despite his departure, McLaren's impressive high-tech headquarters boasts one of the strongest design departments in F1 and the MP4-21 continues Newey's aggressive aerodynamic approach. It's powered by a Mercedes-Benz 2.4-litre V8, which is designed and built in the UK in the former Ilmor factory that the company acquired in 2005. Mercedes also owns 40 percent of McLaren, and the silver paint job recalls the iconic Silver Arrows pre-war racers that dominated Grand Prix racing in the 1930s.

## Statistics

| | |
|---|---|
| **Chassis:** | **Carbon-fibre monocoque** |
| **Engine size:** | **2400cc** |
| **Configuration:** | **V8** |
| **Bhp:** | **750bhp** |
| **Max rpm:** | **19,750rpm** |
| **Top speed:** | **231mph** |
| **0-60mph:** | **2.1sec** |
| **Weight:** | **605kg (inc driver)** |
| **Gearbox:** | **Seven-speed semi-automatic** |
| **Fuel:** | **Mobil 1 unleaded** |
| **Tyres:** | **Michelin** |
| **Wheels:** | **Enkei 13in rims** |
| **Front suspension:** | **Double wishbone with inboard torsion bar/ damper** |
| **Rear suspension:** | **Double wishbone with inboard torsion bar/ damper** |
| **Brakes:** | **Carbon-fibre discs front and rear** |

# DTM
# Mercedes–Benz C-Klasse

**The fastest family saloon in the west**

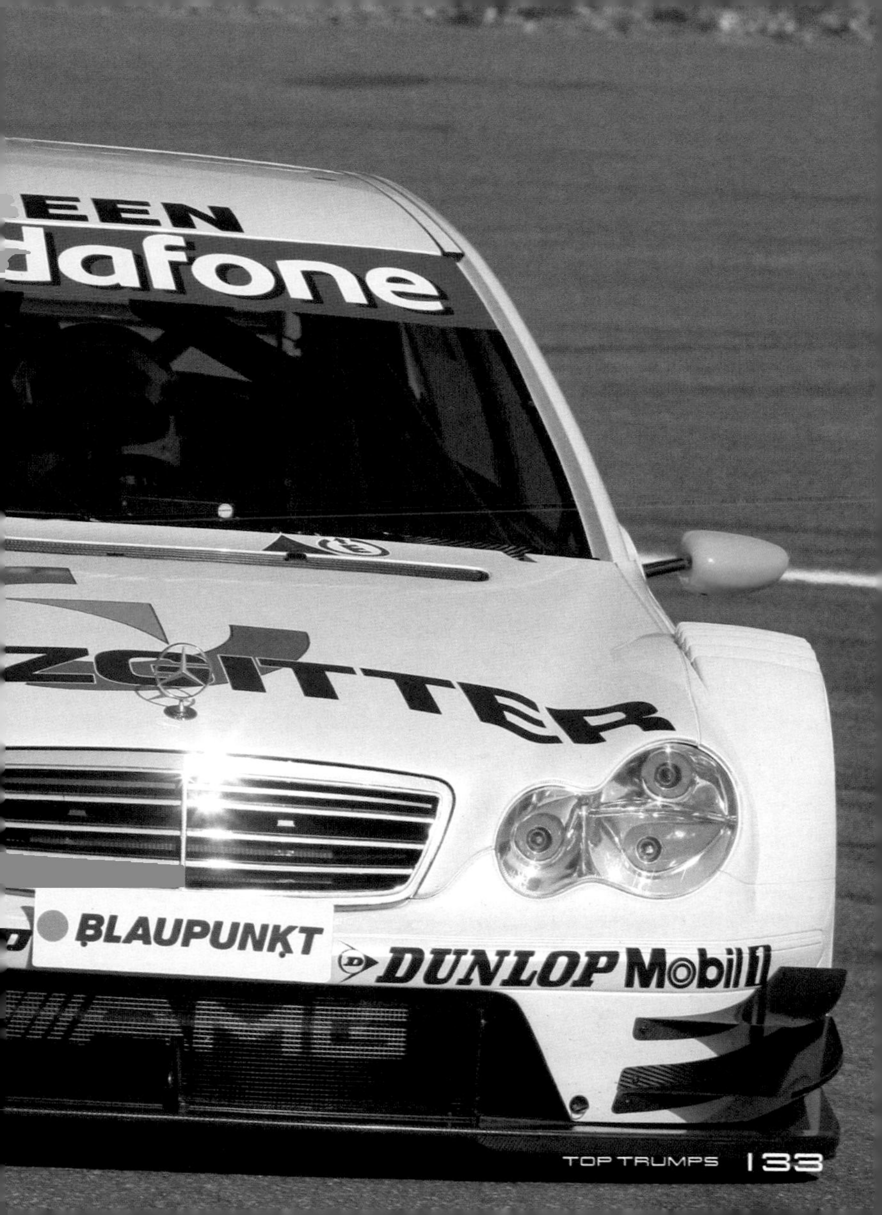
BLAUPUNKT
DUNLOP
Mobil 1

# DTM
# Mercedes-Benz C-Klasse

**The fastest family saloon in the west**

The German-based DTM touring car series is Europe's fastest form of tin-top racing. The championship has existed in numerous guises since 1984, but the current format of V8-powered silhouette four-door saloons has been in place since 2001. Mercedes has been involved in the series since its rebirth and the 475bhp C-Klasse has been the dominant car, taking the 2005 championship. Mercedes' motorsport arm, AMG, designs and builds the car, while the low-revving V8s are the product of HWA. For 2006, the technical specifications of the cars were frozen and the latest version is only a refinement of its title-winning sibling. Multiple DTM champ Bernd Schneider, two-times Formula 1 world title winner Mika Hakkinen and rising British star Jamie Green are the key players in Mercedes' 10-car DTM line-up, which also includes a smattering of 2005 and 2004 machinery.

## Statistics

| | |
|---|---|
| **Chassis:** | **Tubular steel frame** |
| **Engine size:** | **4000cc** |
| **Configuration:** | **V8** |
| **Bhp:** | **470bhp** |
| **Max rpm:** | **7500rpm** |
| **Top speed:** | **170mph** |
| **0-60mph:** | **4.0sec** |
| **Weight:** | **1070kg (inc driver)** |
| **Gearbox:** | **Six-speed sequential** |
| **Fuel:** | **Unleaded** |
| **Tyres:** | **Michelin** |
| **Wheels:** | **BBS 13in rims** |
| **Front suspension:** | **Double wishbone with pushrod-activated torsion springs** |
| **Rear suspension:** | **Double wishbone with pushrod-activated torsion springs** |
| **Brakes:** | **Carbon-fibre discs front and rear** |

# Nissan Fairlady (350Z)

**My Fairlady doesn't need good manners**

# Super GT
# Nissan Fairlady (350Z)

**My Fairlady doesn't need good manners**

For the 2004 season Nissan used the Japan-based Super GT series to promote its new Fairlady model (known as the 350Z in Europe). It replaced the Skyline, which had enjoyed a great deal of success, winning five titles in 12 years. The Fairlady instantly carried on where the Skyline left off and, in the hands of Japanese ace Satoshi Motoyama and Irishman Richard Lyons, took the 2004 title. Like the Skyline, the Fairlady was developed by Nissan's performance arm, NISMO. Super GT rules limit cars in the top GT500 category to 500bhp and Nissan achieves this by the use of a twin turbo 3-litre V6. There are five 350Zs in the GT500 class: two run by Nismo and one each for Hasemi, Impul and Konda Racing. The success ballast regulations of the series ensure that no single car is able to dominate a season, but the 350Z remains a contender at every track visited.

## Statistics

| | |
|---|---|
| Chassis: | Tubular steel frame |
| Engine size: | 2997cc |
| Configuration: | V6 twin turbo |
| Bhp: | 500bhp |
| Max rpm: | 7200rpm |
| Top speed: | 190mph |
| 0-60mph: | 3.8sec |
| Weight: | 1100kg |
| Gearbox: | Six-speed sequential |
| Fuel: | Unleaded |
| Tyres: | Bridgestone/Dunlop |
| Wheels: | 18in rims |
| Front suspension: | Double wishbone |
| Rear suspension: | Double wishbone |
| Brakes: | Steel discs front and rear |

# Le Mans
# Pescarolo–Judd C60

**Legend aims for sportscar glory**

# Pescarolo-Judd C60

**Legend aims for sportscar glory**

Henri Pescarolo is one of the greatest sportscar racers in history and a four-time winner of the Le Mans 24 Hours. In 2000 he established Pescarolo Sport and ran a Courage chassis with the clear aim of once again adding his name to the winners' list of the classic French endurance race. The project originally used Peugeot engines, but that relationship ended after three seasons and for 2004 Judd power was mated to a rebodied Courage C60 chassis. This brought a step forward in competitiveness and a year later, with the car adapted to the revised aerodynamic regulations, the Pescarolo lead car was on pole and took second in the race. For 2006 the crack line-up of Emmanuel Collard and Jean-Christophe Boullion dominated the Le Mans Series, crushing its rivals in the LMP1 category of the championship.

## Statistics

| | |
|---|---|
| **Chassis:** | **Carbon-fibre/ aluminium monocoque** |
| **Engine size:** | **4997cc** |
| **Configuration:** | **V10** |
| **Bhp:** | **630bhp** |
| **Max rpm:** | **7800rpm** |
| **Top speed:** | **215mph** |
| **0-60mph:** | **2.8sec** |
| **Weight:** | **900kg** |
| **Gearbox:** | **Six-speed sequential** |
| **Fuel:** | **Unleaded** |
| **Tyres:** | **Michelin** |
| **Wheels:** | **18in rims** |
| **Front suspension:** | **Double wishbone with pushrods** |
| **Rear suspension:** | **Double wishbone with pushrods** |
| **Brakes:** | **Carbon-fibre discs front and rear** |

# FIA GT
# Porsche GT3 RSR

**The latest in a long line of GT greats**

# FIA GT
# Porsche GT3 RSR

**The latest in a long line of GT greats**

Since the 1960s Porsche has been a mainstay of sportscar and GT racing and its venerable 911 has been almost ever-present in a variety of guises in championships all over the world. Just as Porsche has continued to refine and improve its road-going version of the rear-engined 911, so the racing version has continued to evolve. For 2006, Porsche took a further step forward with the introduction of the GT3 RSR. Somewhat confusingly given its name, the Porsche actually races in the GT2 category in the FIA GT series, where it does battle with the Ferrari 430. The car is an evolution of the model introduced in 2003 and continues to play on Porsche's strengths of remarkable reliability and great handling. It's because of these attributes and Porsche's dedication to its motorsport customers that the 911 continues to be the most successful GT car in the world in terms of sheer numbers.

# Statistics

| | |
|---|---|
| **Chassis:** | Tubular steel frame |
| **Engine size:** | 3598cc |
| **Configuration:** | Flat six |
| **Bhp:** | 455bhp |
| **Max rpm:** | 8700rpm |
| **Top speed:** | 195mph |
| **0-60mph:** | 4.2sec |
| **Weight:** | 1100kg |
| **Gearbox:** | Six-speed sequential |
| **Fuel:** | Mobil 1 unleaded |
| **Tyres:** | Michelin |
| **Wheels:** | BBS 18in rims |
| **Front suspension:** | McPherson strut with adjustable dampers |
| **Rear suspension:** | Multi-link rear axle with adjustable dampers |
| **Brakes:** | Iron discs front and rear |

# Porsche RS
# Spyder LMP2

**Famous partners reunite for sportscar challenge**

# ALMS
# Porsche RS Spyder LMP2

**Famous partners reunite for sportscar challenge**

Porsche is synonymous with sportscars and endurance racing, yet the German manufacturer had shied away from taking on Audi's mighty R8 in sports prototypes in recent years. All that changed in 2005 when it revealed plans to build its first prototype racer since its stillborn 2000 project. The surprise was that this wouldn't be a top-class LMP1 racer, but an LMP2. The theory was two-fold. The LMP2 cars run lighter, and thus could potentially match LMP1 pace; secondly the market for customer cars in this cheaper class was greater. Porsche teamed up with crack US racing outfit Penske for the project, recreating a partnership that had enjoyed great success in the 1970s. They made two outings at the end of 2005 ahead of a full campaign for 2006. The striking LMP2 instantly proved very quick indeed and promised to give Audi's new R10 a strong run for its money.

# Statistics

| | |
|---|---|
| **Chassis:** | **Carbon-fibre monocoque** |
| **Engine size:** | **3400cc** |
| **Configuration:** | **90-degree V8** |
| **Bhp:** | **480bhp** |
| **Max rpm:** | **10,100rpm** |
| **Top speed:** | **210mph** |
| **0-60mph:** | **3.1sec** |
| **Weight:** | **775kg** |
| **Gearbox:** | **Six-speed sequential** |
| **Fuel:** | **Mobil 1 unleaded** |
| **Tyres:** | **Michelin** |
| **Wheels:** | **18in rims** |
| **Front suspension:** | **Double wishbone with adjustable dampers** |
| **Rear suspension:** | **Double wishbone with adjustable dampers** |
| **Brakes:** | **Carbon-fibre discs front and rear** |

# Formula 1
# Red Bull RB2
**Giving wings to an F1 team**

# Formula 1
# Red Bull RB2

**Giving wings to an F1 team**

Red Bull isn't just the world's largest producer of fizzy energy drinks, but it's now also a major player in Formula 1. With Austrian billionaire Dietrich Mateschitz signing the cheques, the company bought a place in F1 when it took over the assets of the Jaguar Racing team at the end of 2004. With this came the Milton Keynes factory, two windtunnels and the R6 chassis Jaguar had prepared for the 2005 season. Ultra-successful Formula 3000 team owner Christian Horner was brought in to run the team and it had a great debut season, scoring more than double the best points haul ever managed by Jaguar. For 2006, the team stepped up a notch and bought in Ferrari 2.4-litre engines in place of Cosworths to power the RB2 and hired aerodynamic ace Adrian Newey from rivals McLaren. The 2005 driver line-up of veteran Scot David Coulthard and Austrian Red Bull driver programme graduate Christian Klien was retained.

# Statistics

| | |
|---|---|
| Chassis: | Carbon-fibre monocoque |
| Engine size: | 2398cc |
| Configuration: | V8 |
| Bhp: | 750bhp |
| Max rpm: | 19,750rpm |
| Top speed: | 231mph |
| 0-60mph: | 2.1sec |
| Weight: | 605kg (inc driver) |
| Gearbox: | Seven-speed semi-automatic |
| Fuel: | Shell unleaded |
| Tyres: | Michelin |
| Wheels: | Avus 13in rims |
| Front suspension: | Double wishbone with pushrods |
| Rear suspension: | Double wishbone with pushrods |
| Brakes: | Carbon-fibre discs front and rear |

# Formula 1
# Renault R26

**The best just got better**

# Formula 1
# Renault R26
**The best just got better**

The Renault R26 is an evolution of the double championship-winning R25. Changes to the Formula 1 engine and tyre regulations forced the Renault engineers to find even more aerodynamic efficiency from what was already a proven race-winning package. The solution has demonstrated to be even better than the car it replaced – it has so many strengths that there's no single area in which it really excels, but Renault's electronic launch control system, which cuts power to the rear wheels to ensure a wheelspin-free getaway, is the class of the field and means World Champion Fernando Alonso and team-mate Giancarlo Fisichella are usually the fastest off the line at the start of a race. The car is designed and built in Enstone, England, while the 2.4-litre V8 engine comes from Viry in France. Despite the distance between the two factories, the pair are perfectly mated, making the R26 the all-round best package in Formula 1 in 2006.

## Statistics

| | |
|---|---|
| **Chassis:** | **Carbon-fibre monocoque** |
| **Engine size:** | **2400cc** |
| **Configuration:** | **V8** |
| **Bhp:** | **750bhp** |
| **Max rpm:** | **19,500rpm** |
| **Top speed:** | **231mph** |
| **0-60mph:** | **2.1sec** |
| **Weight:** | **605kg (inc driver)** |
| **Gearbox:** | **Seven-speed semi-automatic** |
| **Fuel:** | **Elf unleaded** |
| **Tyres:** | **Michelin** |
| **Wheels:** | **OZ 13in rims** |
| **Front suspension:** | **Double wishbone with pushrods** |
| **Rear suspension:** | **Double wishbone with pushrods** |
| **Brakes:** | **Carbon-fibre discs front and rear** |

TEAM SPIRIT

# FIA GT
# Saleen S7R
**Exotic American GT muscle car**

# FIA GT
# Saleen S7R

**Exotic American GT muscle car**

Saleen has been building its unique brand of supercars for over 20 years. During that time it has established a close relationship with Ford, and helped the US car giant with the construction of its GT supercar. This relationship extended to the track, and the thunderous Saleen Mustangs were a crowd favourite wherever they went – and have recorded over 50 class wins in various competitions all over the world. But for 2001, Saleen decided to campaign its own car, the fearsome S7R. The car instantly proved to be quick, but, fast as it was, it was also fragile. Over the years, Saleen and its customers Zakspeed Racing and ORECA have worked hard to make the car last for an entire endurance race, and their efforts have been paying off – the S7R is a genuine threat to the Maserati MC12 and Aston Martin DBR9 in the FIA GT GT1 class.

## Statistics

| | |
|---|---|
| **Chassis:** | **Steel spaceframe** |
| **Engine size:** | **7000cc** |
| **Configuration:** | **V8** |
| **Bhp:** | **600bhp** |
| **Max rpm:** | **8000rpm** |
| **Top speed:** | **201mph** |
| **0-60mph:** | **3.4sec** |
| **Weight:** | **1100kg** |
| **Gearbox:** | **Six-speed sequential** |
| **Fuel:** | **Unleaded** |
| **Tyres:** | **Michelin/Dunlop** |
| **Wheels:** | **17in rims** |
| **Front suspension:** | **Double wishbone** |
| **Rear suspension:** | **Double wishbone** |
| **Brakes:** | **Carbon-fibre discs front and rear** |

# WTCC
# SEAT Leon

**Spanish step up world touring car attack**

SEAT

Red Bull
betandwin
Muller

Telefónica

SEAT

KW
suspension.de

BORBET.com

ADVAN

movistar

# WTCC
# SEAT Leon

**Spanish step up world touring car attack**

SEAT is Spain's only volume car manufacturer and is part of
the huge Volkswagen Automotive Group. SEAT is also VAG's
representative in the World Touring Car Championship. After
enjoying some success with the Toledo model, SEAT gave a debut
to the new Leon model towards the end of 2005. It instantly proved
a more competitive package and for 2006 the attack expanded to an
enormous six-car squad. The line-up was full of star-name drivers:
SEAT regulars Rickard Rydell, Jordi Gené and Peter Terting joined
by Yvan Muller, James Thompson and Gabriele Tarquini – all former
touring car champions. The SEAT is renowned for its strong engine,
but the SEAT Sport-built car is inherently disadvantaged by its bulky
design. Thus the FIA Bureau, which governs the WTCC, granted a
rules break to the Leon's aerodynamic package, allowing the car to
become a genuine challenge to the dominant BMWs.

| | |
|---|---|
| Chassis: | Tubular steel frame |
| Engine size: | 2000cc |
| Configuration: | In-line four |
| Bhp: | 260bhp |
| Max rpm: | 8500rpm |
| Top speed: | 160mph |
| 0-60mph: | 4.0sec |
| Weight: | 1140kg |
| Gearbox: | Six-speed sequential |
| Fuel: | Unleaded |
| Tyres: | Yokohama |
| Wheels: | 17in rims |
| Front suspension: | McPherson strut with adjustable dampers |
| Rear suspension: | Multi-link with adjustable dampers |
| Brakes: | Iron discs front and rear |

# Formula 3
# SLC-Opel
**Brave attempt to take on Dallara in F3**

# Formula 3
# SLC-Opel

**Brave attempt to take on Dallara in F3**

The Super Light Car company wanted to showcase its engineering prowess by designing and constructing an F3 car to rival Dallara. The Italian firm teamed up with well-established French outfit Signature to run the car in the 2005 Euroseries, but, despite having F3 veteran Fabio Carbone in the driving seat, the car struggled to keep pace with the multitude of Dallaras. In initial testing it performed well, but it was hamstrung by reliability problems with its compact gearbox, which came out of Ralt's failed F3 project. With a larger, heavier replacement unit installed, the reliability was sorted, but the aerodynamic advantage brought about by the compact rear end was lost and with more weight at the back the chassis was hard to balance. The Spiess-built Opel engine is a veteran of the series and was bulky compared to the newer Mercedes. Because of this the decision was taken to step back in 2006 and run a pair of cars in the German-based Recaro F3 Cup for 2005-spec cars to allow the project to develop in a less high-profile series.

| | |
|---|---|
| **Chassis:** | **Carbon-fibre monocoque** |
| **Engine size:** | **1998cc** |
| **Configuration:** | **In-line four** |
| **Bhp:** | **210bhp** |
| **Max rpm:** | **6000rpm** |
| **Top speed:** | **175mph** |
| **0-60mph:** | **2.9sec** |
| **Weight:** | **550kg (inc driver)** |
| **Gearbox:** | **Six-speed sequential** |
| **Fuel:** | **Unleaded** |
| **Tyres:** | **Hankook** |
| **Wheels:** | **ATS 13in rims** |
| **Front suspension:** | **Double wishbone with twin dampers** |
| **Rear suspension:** | **Double wishbone with twin dampers** |
| **Brakes:** | **Carbon-fibre discs front and rear** |

# FIA GT
# Spyker C8
# Spyder GT2R
### Going Dutch in GT racing

# FIA GT
# Spyker C8
# Spyder GT2R
**Going Dutch in GT racing**

Spyker is one of those oddities, a Dutch car company. The name dates back to 1898, but the original company ceased trading in 1925. It was resurrected in 2000 and entered the motorsport arena with the C8 Spyder in the 2001 Le Mans 24 Hours. With limited resources, the project was suspended at the end of 2003, but in 2005 the unique open-top GT2 car was back, although for 2006 a hardtop version was raced. A 3.8-litre Audi V8 provided the power and special dispensation was granted to allow the bodywork to be widened, making it more competitive in the GT2 class in endurance races. With improved performance, the works Spyker Squadron (the original company also built planes) recruited a top-notch line-up of drivers as it seeks to establish the brand in the highly-competitive market of exclusive high-speed cars.

# Statistics

| | |
|---|---|
| **Chassis:** | Aluminium spaceframe |
| **Engine size:** | 3799cc |
| **Configuration:** | V8 |
| **Bhp:** | 450bhp |
| **Max rpm:** | 8500rpm |
| **Top speed:** | 187mph |
| **0-60mph:** | 3.8sec |
| **Weight:** | 1100kg |
| **Gearbox:** | Six-speed sequential |
| **Fuel:** | Unleaded |
| **Tyres:** | Michelin |
| **Wheels:** | 17in rims |
| **Front suspension:** | Double wishbone |
| **Rear suspension:** | Double wishbone |
| **Brakes:** | Iron discs front and rear |

# Formula 1
# Toyota TF106

**The sleeping giant awakes**

# Formula 1
# Toyota TF106

**The sleeping giant awakes**

Toyota is the world's richest car manufacturer and has an excellent winning record in most of the forms of motorsport it has tackled. In 2002 it entered Formula 1 for the first time, and with the huge resources at its disposal, great success was anticipated. But inside the team the project began with modest expectations, although it did score points on its very first outing. Since then it has taken gradual steps forward and in 2005 it achieved its first pole position, which was soon followed by its first podium. This led to greater expectations and a huge development programme on the 2006 car – the TF106 – at the team's enormous Cologne headquarters, where two wind tunnel aerodynamic programmes run simultaneously. The chassis design was overseen by technical director Mike Gascoyne, but when early-season results failed to match expectations he was suspended from the role. The team's driver pairing of Ralf Schumacher and Jarno Trulli is one of the most experienced on the current F1 grid.

# Statistics

| | |
|---|---|
| **Chassis:** | **Carbon-fibre monocoque** |
| **Engine size:** | **2398cc** |
| **Configuration:** | **V8** |
| **Bhp:** | **750bhp** |
| **Max rpm:** | **19,500rpm** |
| **Top speed:** | **230mph** |
| **0-60mph:** | **2.1sec** |
| **Weight:** | **605kg (inc driver)** |
| **Gearbox:** | **Seven-speed semi-automatic** |
| **Fuel:** | **Unleaded** |
| **Tyres:** | **Bridgestone** |
| **Wheels:** | **13in rims** |
| **Front suspension:** | **Double wishbone with inboard torsion bar/damper** |
| **Rear suspension:** | **Double wishbone with inboard torsion bar/damper** |
| **Brakes:** | **Carbon-fibre discs front and rear** |

## BTCC

# Vauxhall Astra

**Ex-champions push forward with new car**

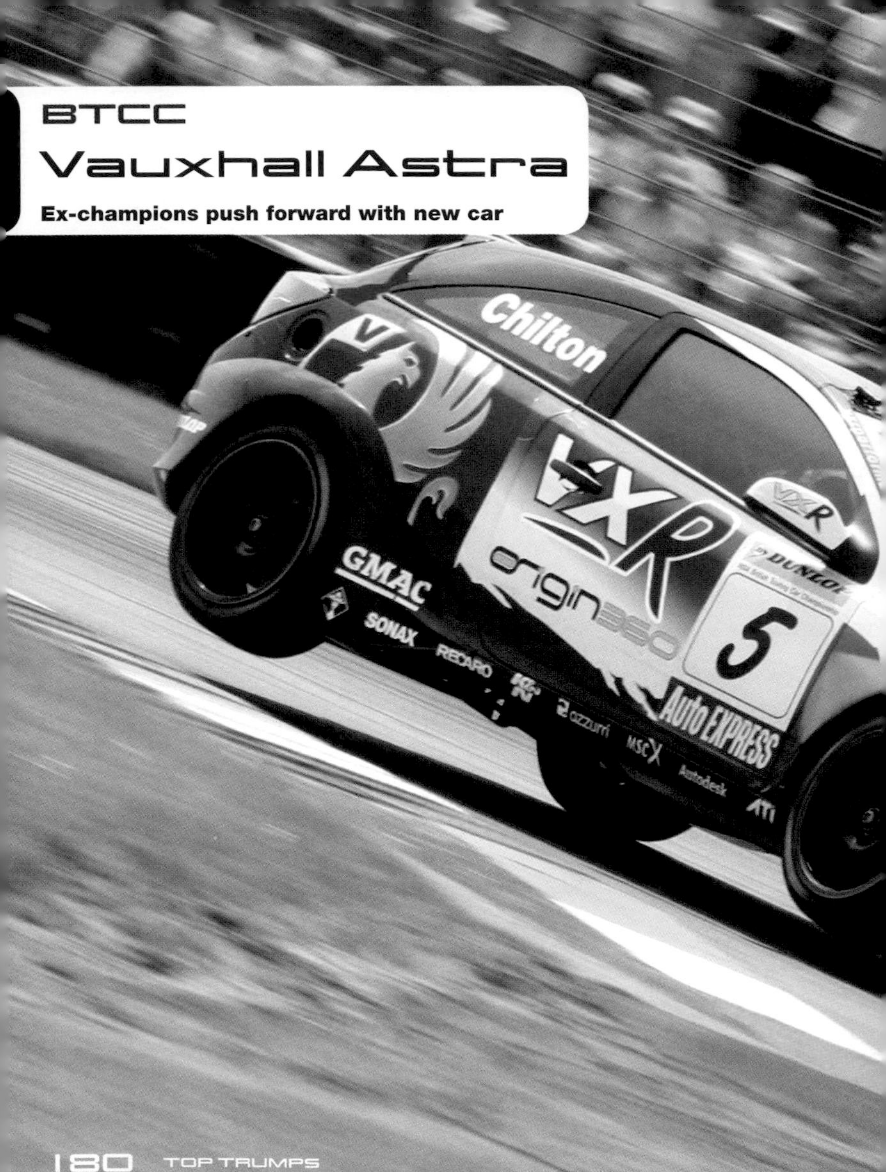

# BTCC
# Vauxhall Astra

**Ex-champions push forward with new car**

Vauxhall has been the dominant force in the British Touring Car
Championship since the current low-cost rules were introduced
in 2001. The BTCC regs are close to the Super 2000 ones used in
the WTCC, but differ slightly in terms of engine spec, suspension
and aerodynamic restrictions. Triple Eight Engineering built
a formidable racer in the Astra Coupé, but when the car was
replaced by the new Astra model, it was forced to develop the
Sports Hatch into a BTCC racer. In 2005 it lost the title for the first
time in the new era, and so adopted an aggressive development
strategy over winter testing. This included bringing in two new
drivers – multiple touring car title winner Fabrizio Giovanardi came
from Alfa's WTCC programme, while Tom Chilton is the most
spectacular young talent of the series. French engine specialist
Sodemo continue to develop the engine, which is among the most
powerful in the championship.

## Statistics

| | |
|---|---|
| **Chassis:** | Tubular space frame |
| **Engine size:** | 2000cc |
| **Configuration:** | In-line four |
| **Bhp:** | 290bhp |
| **Max rpm:** | 8500rpm |
| **Top speed:** | 160mph |
| **0-60mph:** | 4sec |
| **Weight:** | 1175kg |
| **Gearbox:** | Six-speed sequential |
| **Fuel:** | Unleaded |
| **Tyres:** | Dunlop |
| **Wheels:** | Rimstock 17in rim |
| **Front suspension:** | Double wishbone with adjustable dampers |
| **Rear suspension:** | Torsion beam |
| **Brakes:** | Iron discs front and rear |

# Formula 1
# Williams FW27

**Latest racer from veteran British team**

# Formula 1
# Williams FW27

**Latest racer from veteran British team**

Williams is one of Formula 1's most successful ever teams, although its greatest periods were in the 1980s and 1990s. The new century hasn't not been kind to Sir Frank Williams' outfit. A tie-in with German engine manufacturer BMW failed to yield the expected results and the partnership was severed at the end of 2005. The team also suffered on the technical side too, with the infamous 'walrus' stub-nosed car of 2004 being a high-profile failure. For 2006, the team has gone back to basics with the FW27. Cosworth's high-revving 2.4-litre V8 has been installed into an efficient chassis overseen by team co-owner and engineering genius Patrick Head and his technical director Sam Michael. Australian Mark Webber stayed on for a second season with the Grove-based team, while 2005 GP2 champion Nico Rosberg (son of 1982 F1 World Champ Keke Rosberg) became the team's hot new young charger.

# Statistics

| | |
|---|---|
| **Chassis:** | Carbon-fibre monocoque |
| **Engine size:** | 2398cc |
| **Configuration:** | V8 |
| **Bhp:** | 750bhp |
| **Max rpm:** | 20,000rpm |
| **Top speed:** | 231mph |
| **0-60mph:** | 2.1sec |
| **Weight:** | 605kg (inc driver) |
| **Gearbox:** | Seven-speed semi-automatic |
| **Fuel:** | Petrobras unleaded |
| **Tyres:** | Bridgestone |
| **Wheels:** | 13in rims |
| **Front suspension:** | Double wishbone with pushrods |
| **Rear suspension:** | Double wishbone with pushrods |
| **Brakes:** | Carbon-fibre discs front and rear |

# Checklist

 **Alfa Romeo 156 • WTCC**
Date                    Location

 **Aston Martin DBR9 • FIA GT**
Date                    Location

 **Audi A4 • DTM**
Date                    Location

 **Audi R10 • Le Mans**
Date                    Location

 **BMW 320si • WTCC**
Date                    Location

 **BMW-Sauber F1.06 • Formula 1**
Date                    Location

 **Chevrolet Corvette C6.R • FIA GT**
Date                    Location

 **Chevrolet Lacetti • WTCC**
Date                    Location

 **Chevrolet Monte Carlo • NASCAR**
Date                    Location

 **Dallara-Honda • IRL**
Date                    Location

### Dallara-Mercedes F306 • Formuls 3

**Date**                        **Location**

### Dallara-Renault • GP2

**Date**                        **Location**

### Dallara-Renault • World Series

**Date**                        **Location**

### Daytona Prototype • Grand Am

**Date**                        **Location**

### Dodge Charger • NASCAR

**Date**                        **Location**

### Ferrari F248 • Formula I

**Date**                        **Location**

### Ford Falcon • V8 Supercars

**Date**                        **Location**

### Ford Fusion • NASCAR

**Date**                        **Location**

### Grand Prix • Masters

**Date**                        **Location**

### Holden Commodore • V8 Supercars

**Date**                        **Location**

### Honda Integra-R • BTCC

**Date**                        **Location**

## Honda NSX • Super GT
**Date** **Location**

## Honda RA106 • Formula 1
**Date** **Location**

## Lamborghini Murcielago R-GT • FIA GT
**Date** **Location**

## Lexus SC430 • Super GT
**Date** **Location**

## Lola-Ford • Champ Car
**Date** **Location**

## Lola FN06 • Formula Nippon
**Date** **Location**

## Lola-Mugen B06/30 • Formula 3
**Date** **Location**

## Lola-Zytek • A1 Grand Prix
**Date** **Location**

## Maserati MC12 • FIA GT
**Date** **Location**

## McLaren MP4-21 • Formula 1
**Date** **Location**

## Mercedes C-Klasse • DTM
**Date** **Location**

## Nissan Fairlady (350Z) • Super GT
**Date** **Location**

## Pescarolo-Judd C60 • Le Mans

**Date**                        **Location**

## Porsche GT3 RSR • FIA GT

**Date**                        **Location**

## Porsche RS Spyder LMP2 • ALMS

**Date**                        **Location**

## Red Bull RB2 • Formula 1

**Date**                        **Location**

## Renault R26 • Formula 1

**Date**                        **Location**

## Saleen S7R • FIA GT

**Date**                        **Location**

## SEAT Leon • WTCC

**Date**                        **Location**

## SLC-Opel • Formula 3

**Date**                        **Location**

## Spyker C8 Spyder GT2R • FIA GT

**Date**                        **Location**

## Toyota TF106 • Formula 1

**Date**                        **Location**

## Vauxhall Astra • BTCC

**Date**                        **Location**

## Williams FW27 • Formula 1

**Date**                        **Location**